EVOLVING LEADERS

A MODEL FOR PROMOTING LEADERSHIP DEVELOPMENT IN PROGRAMS

EVOLVING LEADERS

A MODEL FOR PROMOTING LEADERSHIP DEVELOPMENT IN PROGRAMS

Charles J. Palus
Wilfred H. Drath

Center for Creative Leadership
Greensboro, North Carolina

The Center for Creative Leadership is an international, nonprofit educational institution founded in 1970 to foster leadership and effective management for the good of society overall. As a part of this mission, it publishes books and reports that aim to contribute to a general process of inquiry and understanding in which ideas related to leadership are raised, exchanged, and evaluated. The ideas presented in its publications are those of the author or authors.

The Center thanks you for supporting its work through the purchase of this volume. If you have comments, suggestions, or questions about any Center publication, please contact Walter W. Tornow, Vice President, Research and Publication, at the address given below.

Center for Creative Leadership
Post Office Box 26300
Greensboro, North Carolina 27438-6300

CENTER FOR CREATIVE LEADERSHIP

©1995 Center for Creative Leadership

CCL No. 165

Library of Congress Cataloging-in-Publication Data

Palus, Charles J.
    Evolving leaders : a model for promoting leadership development in programs /
Charles J. Palus, Wilfred H. Drath.
        p.   cm.
    Includes bibliographical references (p.   ).
    ISBN 1-882197-11-9
    1. Leadership. 2. Leadership—Study and teaching. 3. Executives—Training of.
4. Leadership—Case studies. I. Drath, Wilfred H. II. Title.
    HD57.7.P35 1995
    658.4'07124—dc20   95-36809
                                                                            CIP

Table of Contents

Acknowledgments

To the many people who helped us shape the ideas in this paper, we give our thanks. We especially thank the following people for their support, input, and helpful criticisms: Michael Basseches, Robert Burnside, Maxine Dalton, Nancy Dixon, Robert Fulmer, Stan Gryskiewicz, Michael Hoppe, Marcia Horowitz, David Horth, Winn Legerton, Abigail Lipson, Cindy McCauley, Glenn Mehltretter, Jr., Sharon Rogolsky, Judy Rosenblum, Marian Ruderman, Sylvester Taylor, Walt Tornow, Ellen Van Velsor, Martin Wilcox, and Dianne Young.

Preface

We should say a bit about the background of this paper.

In 1991 a team, which included the first author, began a research project to assess a new Center program called LeaderLab®. We wanted to look at more than the teaching and learning of competencies, to see the program in relation to the subtlety and complexity of human growth, adaptation, and change. We realized that development programs are not the only influence on the growth of participants; work, family, community, and self are also factors. We were, in addition, interested in the idea of readiness for development—that people differ in how ready they are to develop—as previously raised by Chris Musselwhite and Ellen Van Velsor (Musselwhite, 1985; Van Velsor & Musselwhite, 1986) in their studies of the Center's "Leadership Development Program." With all these complexities, it seemed important to us to "break set" and see the new program in new ways. That is when we first conceived of the model presented in this paper.

Around the same time, the second author published an article (Drath, 1990) that made use of the adult developmental framework of Robert Kegan (1982). This interpretation of the life experiences of senior executives in the Awareness Program for Executive Excellence (APEX)® connected the work of the Center to that of the study of adult life span development, a connection further explored in the present paper.

Also around that time the staff of the Center engaged in a lengthy dialogue on whether we should endorse and disseminate a definition of leadership. Ultimately it was decided not to adopt any single definition (because the range of Center activities, from training to research, makes it impractical to have just one), but that discussion helped us develop a new understanding of leadership (see Drath & Palus, 1994). That led naturally to a new way of understanding leadership development.

The model in this report is currently being used by a team designing a new organizational simulation. The simulation is envisioned as a tool that will help participants develop by having them respond to scenarios representative of emerging organizational issues. The team, which includes both authors, has had to stretch itself in thinking about the nature of leadership and about how its development may be facilitated. Its work has enriched the content of this report.

We want to emphasize that this paper is not an exposition of "the way things are." The study of leadership resists demonstrations of enduring truths.

It would serve our dialogue with you, the reader, much better if you would consider this paper an invitation to join us in thinking, "What if . . . ?" What if we ponder leadership and leadership development in certain new ways? What then happens to our sense and practice of it? What do we encounter and discover? What might we be missing in our present perceptions? This approach seems most sensible, as the horizon of the future is coming right at us, as we reframe our organizations and ponder the way things might be.

For this *invitational mood* of language we owe the psychologist George Kelly, who contrasted the statement, "The floor is hard" with the statement, "Suppose we regard the floor as if it were hard" (Kelly, 1969, pp. 148-149; see also Korzybski, 1941). The former seems obvious and not worth discussing. Case closed. The latter

> leaves both the speaker and the listener, not with a conclusion on their hands, but in a posture of expectancy . . . . It suggests the floor is open to a variety of interpretations or constructions. (Kelly, 1969, p. 149)

> Out of this further exploration may come, not so much confirmation that it is really hard or that it is really soft . . . but a sequence of fresh experiences that invite the formulation of new hypotheses. For example, one may come up with a notion of relativism, that is to say, the floor is harder than some things and softer than others. . . . He may launch out and contrive the notions of resilience and plasticity to account for what happened when he treated the floor as if it were soft. (Kelly, 1969, p. 160)

Please join us, then, in a train of thought, "a sequence of fresh experiences." We ask that you *not* surrender your current ideas about leadership and leadership development. (After all, "The floor is hard" remains a highly useful concept.) Your own hard-won ideas in these matters will surely add to what we have to say.

Introduction

Although leadership development is widely acknowledged as important, our understanding of it is largely implicit. This has made programs that seek to promote it difficult to design and implement, and challenging to evaluate effectively.

In this paper we will present an explicit model of how leadership development can be promoted using programs. We are speaking here primarily to people who are responsible for leadership development in organizations or who design or evaluate programs. The model, however, should also be of interest to researchers who are studying leadership and to practicing leaders who are seeking to understand their own development.

Perspective and Focus

Because the model we present here is the product of a distinct view of leadership and development, we should briefly describe our perspective (see Drath & Palus, 1994).

Historically, leadership has been understood in terms of dominance and influence: An individual called a *leader* acts in some way to change the behavior or attitudes of others called *followers*. We think that this notion of leadership can be seen within a larger context, one which includes more general social processes. In brief, we regard leadership *as meaning-making in a community of practice*: People engaged in a shared activity make sense of their experience together so that they can communicate, cooperate, and agree about what is happening, and so that they can interpret, anticipate, plan, and act. From this perspective it is possible to see the common underlying leadership processes in a range of situations from dictatorships to so-called leaderless work groups.

Also from this perspective, leadership development takes on a different look. It is usually seen as an almost exclusively individual process in which a leader gains additional skills to influence followers. If leadership is understood as a social activity, though, then leadership development must involve some change in the collective activity, in addition to some change in individuals.

More specifically, any meaning structure (or interpretation, construction) that a community uses to make sense of things will eventually come up against something that it cannot handle. The process of adaptation takes place as people try to collectively evolve a new meaning structure that can explain the changed conditions. It involves the development of the leadership process and can thus be included in the idea of leadership development (Heifetz, 1994).

The adaptive processes of leadership development can happen in three ways: when new forms of practice are created; when people are brought into new ways of relating to others in the community; and when individual members develop psychologically. Our model in this paper deals primarily with the last of these—individual psychological development—in light of the requirements of the first two.

Thus, our focus is on the use of programs to enhance the growth of the individual's ability to participate in the leadership processes of the community of practice.

We are concentrating on that aspect here because we believe that individual development is a key component of leadership development. Also, the use of programs in support of individual leader development is common and widely valued, even if poorly understood.

Before we can say how individual psychological development (and, through it, leadership development) can be promoted in a program, we have to say more about individual development in general.

Just as communities create meaning structures to make sense of their experience, so do individuals. We take the position that, typically, for each of us there is one meaning structure that organizes and comprehends all the others. Jean Piaget (1954) referred to this metastructure as an "epistemology." Throughout our lives we evolve a succession of such structures, which may therefore be thought of as stages of development (there are also smaller, partial, or more idiosyncratic shifts in meaning structure within the larger wholes). According to this view, there is a general pattern to development, such that everyone tends to go through the same stages in the same order.

A key concept of stage development is that each stage is qualitatively distinct but depends on—and, in fact, incorporates and transcends—the previous one.[1] Later stages are built upon earlier ones: A person must sufficiently address the inherent tasks of earlier stages to ensure success in later stages (Erikson, 1963). The abilities of earlier stages may remain available, but in ways that are reorganized and coordinated by the later stage.

As a simple example of stages of development, consider the sequence involved in learning how to walk, illustrated in Figure 1.[2] At first the infant is immobile. A step change occurs when it is able to repeatedly organize its movements in order to roll. This has a revolutionary effect: The infant's experience of the world becomes fundamentally reorganized by its ability to roll around in it. Likewise, crawling is a reorganization of movement that has a profound effect on experience. And so on, with walking, then running.

Stage		Mobility
4	↑	Running
3	|	Walking
2	|	Crawling
1	|	Rolling
0	|	Static

Figure 1. A Stage Developmental Model of Learning to Walk
(adapted from Boydell, Leary, Megginson, & Pedler, 1991)

Distinctions

This view of development makes it possible to distinguish between development and something it is often confused or equated with: learning. When a single new insight or piece of information is assimilated into the underlying frameworks of one's current stage, this can be understood as learning. Sometimes, however, the stage cannot adequately assimilate new information, and a new stage that is more encompassing is generated to better organize complex and diverse information. This process of accommodation— more specifically, reorganization of one's epistemology—is the essential motion of development (Piaget, 1954).[3]

It also allows us to draw a distinction between training programs and development programs. A training program attempts to impart skills within a person's existing stage of development. A program that teaches a person to type is a simple example of a training program. A development program, in comparison, helps a person stretch toward a qualitatively new set of meaning structures, toward a new stage (Boydell, Leary, Megginson, & Pedler, 1991).

A development program may also help a person acquire skills but in ways that challenge his or her overall ways of making meaning. Thus "going to college" is an example of a development program (Perry, 1970): Individual classes may involve only learning or training, but the entire course of study (if successful) imparts a comprehensive new meaning structure. Of course, the distinction between training programs and development programs is rarely clear-cut, because training and development interpenetrate: Rigorous training tends to stretch a person's frameworks, and development requires the learning of new skills.

The Model

The model we offer (see Figure 2) shows a cyclic process of three time-linked categories: readiness for development, developmental processes, and outcomes. At first glance these categories might not seem different from those used in training for the learning of specific content. As we discuss the makeup of these categories and their processes, it should be clear that we are concerned not so much with imparting skills but with the evolution of more encompassing and adaptive meaning structures.[4]

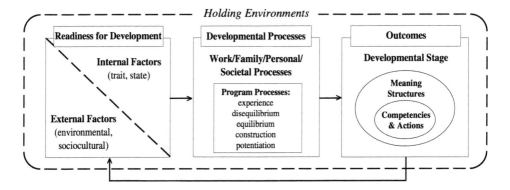

Figure 2. Leadership Development Program Model

Readiness for Development

The term *readiness for development* refers to a simple and important observation: There are developmental differences among people entering leadership development programs, and within an individual at different points in his or her life. The basic diagnostic question for readiness is, "What kind of developmental work is each person best prepared to do?" Or perhaps, "Where are they at, what do they need, and how do they need it?" Adding to the complexity introduced by this basic observation is a related point: There will be cultural differences in the supportiveness of the home environments (organizational, familial, societal) for these differing developmental positions. And this: Some people will be well-prepared to engage a potentially stressful developmental experience; others will not be ready for additional stress in their lives. Some strategy for comprehending and handling diverse needs within the program context, including screening and sorting participants, is necessary.

We propose four types of readiness factors: trait, state, environmental, and sociocultural. Trait and state refer to a person's internal condition. Environmental and sociocultural refer to a person's external milieu. Table 1 lists selected factors we propose for each type. Two cautions are in order. First, although it can be useful to focus on the role of various specific readiness factors—as a diagnostic strategy, in research, or in a process of programmatic feedback—it must be kept in mind that the diagnosis of readiness involves a consideration of the pattern which is emergent from the totality of factors—that is, consideration of the "whole person"—rather than of abstract factors taken one at a time. And, second, there is typically a great deal of interdependence among these four types of readiness factors, and distinctions among the types are not always clear-cut. For example, a person's age is a state that is laden with sociocultural significance. This typology is meant to be a heuristic device with which to draw more elements into a perception of the patterned whole.

Table 1. A Selected List of Proposed Developmental Readiness Factors

INTERNAL

Trait	*State*
enduring character	developmental stage
chronic problems	stability of life structure
	life-story
	age
	satisfaction
	acute problems

EXTERNAL

Environmental	*Sociocultural*
holding environments: work, family, community	developmental norms: age, gender, race, class, ethnicity
job challenges	social milieu / world events and conditions
stressful events	
fortuitous events	

Our present understanding of readiness is far from complete; diagnosis of readiness is still more of an art than a science. The following discussion is selective and often speculative. We invite readers to build on our understanding.

Trait readiness factors. By *traits* we mean relatively enduring psychological characteristics of the individual. Traits typically don't change much over time, although the way a trait is expressed is subject to learning and development. For example, introversion/extraversion is an enduring trait dimension, and introversion is identifiable in infancy and tends to persist throughout adulthood (Kagan, 1971; McCrae & Costa, 1984). However, an introverted person may learn to moderate introverted behavior as appropriate, and may become adept at, and more valuing of, extraverted behavior.

What "character" is and how enduring it is is a matter of many alternative definitions and much debate. William James (1890) saw it as that which is "set like plaster" by about age 30. Freud held the die to be cast by age seven or so, the routine fate of adulthood being to relive early patterns. Much developmental theory is at odds with the more extreme versions of "plaster theory." What we are interested in is how a person's character traits affect the development of meaning-making—the substantial aspect of a person which need not harden.

Kaplan (1990, 1991) and his colleagues (Kaplan, Drath, & Kofodimos, 1991) have described a trait that is apparent in high-achieving executives called *expansiveness*: an aggressive need for mastery and the urge to "expand" one's domains. A kind of readiness is revealed in the observation that expansive executives tend to become elevated and isolated by their position, such that they become insulated from valid and useful feedback from others. Thus, an effective intervention has been to flood the individual with data in a supportive yet challenging program context so that any case for change is made comprehensively and convincingly.

Drath (1990) argued that expansive executives tend to be in what Kegan (1982) has called the "Institutional Stage" of development (a stage that features a strong sense of individualized personal identity). Thus strengths, weaknesses, and opportunities for growth derive from a developmental logic that includes "expansive character" as but one element. In this view, some aspects of character that appear to be set in plaster are in fact plastic, and there is the potential for further development.

Palus and his colleagues analyzed the case of Dodge Morgan, a CEO who quit his job in order to pursue his dream of sailing around the world alone. The authors looked at the circumstances that led this consummate expansive into—and then away from—meaning structures oriented toward individual achievement (Palus, Nasby, & Easton, 1991). A life-story perspective (mentioned below) was used to examine readiness in this case study.

A trait that shows promise as a readiness factor is called *openness to experience* (hereafter referred to as *openness*). High openness is characterized by a flexible and inviting (hence "open") approach to new ideas and new experiences. Costa and McCrae (1978) described openness as "marked by toleration for and exploration of the unfamiliar, a playful approach to ideas and problem solving, and an appreciation of experience for its own sake" (p. 127). Openness has been shown to be moderately correlated to the ego-developmental stage as measured on Loevinger's scale (McCrae & Costa, 1990), and to the stage of moral reasoning as measured on Rest's (1979) scale (Rybash, 1982). The trait of openness, at least in some modest amount, would appear to be favorable to the evolution of a person's meaning structures.

Musselwhite (1985) described a constellation of traits, quite similar to openness, which contributed to increased "readiness for learning" in a study of outcomes of a leadership development program. He used the descriptor "facilitator of change" to describe a person who is "innovative, ready to explore, plow new ground," "not a defensive person who hopes to maintain the status quo" (pp. 79, 106).

But high openness is not necessarily desirable: "Individuals [with] excessively high levels of openness may be so easily drawn to each new idea or belief that they are unable to form a coherent and integrated life structure" (McCrae & Costa, in press, p. 31). It does appear that some capacity for openness—and a modest capacity may be sufficient—must be mobilized or "spoken to" during a leadership development program.

Interesting research questions abound: Can openness itself be changed by a transformative experience (Palus, 1993)? Does openness promote the examination and revision of imperatives from childhood (Gould, 1978)? Are open individuals more likely to periodically reshape their life structures (Levinson, Darrow, Klein, Levinson, & McKee, 1978)?

The literature of psychology is filled with descriptions of afflictions that often prove to be more-or-less enduring traits—one might consider these chronic problems—which play havoc with the individual evolution of meaning structures. Chronic schizophrenia is an extreme example of a persistent impairment that is likely to interfere with leadership development. A discussion of this literature, however, is beyond the scope of this paper. Some screening method for severe psychological problems (such as the *Minnesota Multiphasic Personality Inventory*, interpreted by a trained clinician) is appropriate when the methods of the program are particularly stressful, prolonged, and intrusive.

We have just scratched the surface with respect to traits and readiness. Any dimension purported to be an enduring psychological trait may conceivably be viewed in relation to readiness—that is, in relation to where the person is and what he or she needs developmentally. However, the research relating traits to developmental readiness is sparse. The best approach may be a clinical one in which rich data is collected with an effort to understand the whole person, including how one's enduring traits affect evolving structures of personal meaning, as well as the collective meanings in which the person participates.

State readiness factors. State readiness factors are changing characteristics of the individual that influence readiness for development. While the term *trait* emphasizes the "entity" or constant aspects of individual being, the term *state* emphasizes the "process" or changing aspects of individual being. Because development is itself a process, it is more directly dependent upon state than trait readiness factors. Indeed, as Table 1 indicates, there are more state factors than trait factors that can currently be identified as pertinent to developmental readiness.

Developmental stage is itself an important readiness factor. There is merit in the idea of targeting a program to a stage-homogeneous (or roughly so) audience, so that common issues can be addressed directly. Alternatively, deep differences in stages among participants in a program may itself be used as a source of the disequilibrium (see below) necessary for development.

William Perry's (1970, 1981) scheme of developmental positions (or stages) has been used extensively, especially with college learners, to stretch—but not deny—the epistemology (or meta meaning-structure) of the learner (for instance, Moore, 1989).

The stability of one's stage of development is a readiness factor. For example, a person may be in an unstable developmental state by virtue of just entering or just leaving a stage. Developmental needs at each of these points are quite different: A person entering a stage cautiously embraces perspectives that a person leaving that stage repudiates (Lahey, Souvaine, Kegan, Goodman, & Felix, 1985). Appearances may be deceiving: A person might appear, to themselves and others, to be in a stable developmental position but in fact be ripe (with respect to other readiness factors) for substantial change. Obvious disruption, such as a major job change or crisis, divorce, or an illness, *may* be an opportunity for the restructuring of meaning. Because a crisis includes danger as well as opportunity, it is not enough to notice a state of developmental stability or instability without reference to the whole picture, as partly revealed by other readiness factors.

The state of satisfaction with various aspects of life may be understood as a readiness factor. Global dissatisfaction often indicates an opening for new perspectives. Satisfaction is often to some degree a barrier to new perspectives. But as with stability, a person may feel satisfied and yet by other indications (other readiness factors) be ripe for developmental movement.

Chronological age is related to readiness in two ways. Age is a gross predictor of stage, and some particular ages are associated with transition. Consider Erikson's developmental schema, in which biological, psychological, and social demands intersect to produce stages with broad age norms. For example, the tasks of "the Generativity Stage" (such as producing, reproducing, and providing) typically fall into the middle decades of the life span (Erikson, 1963). The pinnacle of generativity is closely connected in our society with Kegan's (1982) "Institutional Stage"—that is, seeing the world with the lens of a strong personal identity. Erikson's final stage, "the Integrity Stage," is identified with late-middle to old age, a time for review and integration, and taking on the roles of the elder—including the objectification and possible transcendence of personal identity. This meaning structure is similar to that of Kegan's "Interindividual Stage," suggesting that while it may be typically found in later life, it need not be limited to that age period.

Daniel Levinson and his colleagues (1978) postulated a number of age ranges in which transitions in life structure were likely (that is, ages 17-22, 28-33, 40-45, 50-55, 60-65). Palus (1993) found clusterings of transformative life experiences reported around ages 30, 40, and 50 and concluded that social expectations frame these "decade age markers" as a kind of developmental precipice, establishing in some cases a self-fulfilling prophecy for transition. Gail Sheehy's popular book *Passages* (1976) has served to reinforce such expectations, making it even more likely that people crossing into a new decade will feel ready (or feel pressured) for development.

Lives are in many ways like stories, sometimes so much so that the "script" of one's life story indicates periods of developmental readiness (Gergen & Gergen, 1987; McAdams, 1988). McAdams asserts that people know their own lives as stories. Some people are self-conscious about these stories, and some are able to sense the necessity of a new "chapter." Or one might look at a person's life story and see a history of development and infer that further development is likely. An individual's personal theory of development is thus of interest to readiness (and it is an underexplored facet of life-story theory and research).

One aspect of personal identity as a story is what Levinson et al. (1978, p. 91) called "the Dream": a "personal myth, an imagined drama," "a vision." Consider the dream of Dodge Morgan, the CEO who quit his job, built a boat, and sailed around the world, nonstop and alone. Morgan lived for twenty years with his dream, a promise to himself that he would someday make a "very significant sail alone with a boat built specifically for the job" (Palus et al., 1991, p. 16). Not only did Morgan's dream culminate in a major transition in his external condition and his activities, but his meaning structures also appeared to undergo a profound shift—all in tune with an identifiable life story.

Finally, we wish to mention the role of some acute problem as a state readiness factor. A person who is temporarily under the malaise of severe anxiety or depression is not a good candidate for a powerful development program that deliberately introduces an element of disequilibrium into a person's perspectives. Of course, such a condition may represent the disequilibrium of development-in-progress, in which case the person probably needs a "natural" or clinical therapeutic milieu (Kegan, 1982) rather than a leadership program.

It would be a mistake to look only at the internal, psychological condition of the individual when considering readiness for development. External factors are of substantial importance. We divide these external factors into the categories of environmental and sociocultural. The former refers to factors in the immediate environment of the individual. The latter refers to more general factors.

Environmental readiness factors. Developmental stages are more than just individually situated perspectives. According to Kegan (1982, p. 116), stages are "held"—validated, echoed, and supported in various ways—by holding environments, consisting of various milieus of the workplace, family, community, and society (see also Winnicott, 1965). The "individual" is more than that; a person is at the same time an "embeddual" (that is, one who is embedded) and made whole and buoyant and meaningful (or not) according to how well the holding environment is holding.

Meaning structures reside in the environment as well as in the individual. You can offer someone a new meaning structure, but structures are embedded in environments as well as in minds, and so environments as well as minds must change. This focus on development draws our attention not only to the workplace but also to other holding environments—other realms of meaning-making that might be able to support and affirm new meanings.

Well-functioning holding environments also "let go"—that is, they recognize and support development in the form of timely emergence and separation. For example, parents support their child within a web of relationship that defines his or her being. These same parents firmly insist that the painful separation of leaving home is to be endured in the face of various manifestations of loss of meaning (such as homesickness, religious crisis, and identity crisis). This separation eventually culminates in a new mode of self-authorship and autonomous identity, and their offspring finds new holding environments for this new meaning structure within specific work and social organizations.

Torbert (1987) reported that organizations seemed supportive, to varying degrees, of "Interpersonal" and "Institutional" stages (in Kegan's, 1982, terms), as well as an intermediate stage Torbert calls the "Technician Stage." The "Institutional Stage," in which one is subject to the meanings of self-authorship and identity, appears to be currently upheld as an ideal by most organizations—and yet there is a growing need for the competencies supported by stages beyond this. Readiness for advanced development in individuals is thus facilitated by organizations—as well as by familial, personal, and community relationships—which have the ability to hold meaning beyond the "Institutional Stage."

The significance of holding environments is paramount in our model of leadership development and not limited to readiness. We will revisit the concept of holding environments below as we discuss the processes and outcomes of development.

The nature of a person's job challenges, particularly certain kinds of changes in type and degree of job challenge, contribute to readiness for development (McCauley, Ruderman, Ohlott, & Morrow, 1994). In a study of the self-reported outcomes of a leadership development program, Musselwhite (1985) identified a number of job-challenge-based readiness factors. Promotions and major changes in responsibility that occurred *before* the leadership development program were seen by participants as beneficial to the impact of the program, whereas the same events occurring *after* the program distracted from the impact of the program. In particular, moving into a management role for the first time, moving into an executive role for the first time, and being newly appointed as president or CEO typically required a substantial shift in perspective (see also Kaplan, Drath, & Kofodimos, 1985) and accentuated readiness for the program. Finally, Musselwhite identified a group that felt that readiness stemmed from a *lack of* a personally significant job challenge, including burnout and what has been described as a midlife identity crisis.

The occurrence of various kinds of stressful events can affect readiness in two possible ways. First, accumulated life stress might bring a person to the point where new meaning structures are embraced in order to cope (Lazarus, 1966; Taylor, 1989). However, the same amount of stress in another person might place them in a fragile state, one that does not warrant the additional stress of a developmental program. To our knowledge research has not been done that would resolve this individual difference, and again we suggest that this factor be dealt with in the context of all available information on readiness.

The second way in which a stress may influence readiness is as a single event which sends a person down a particular road of life's possibilities. For example, being laid off from one's job may lead to a new circle of friends and new holding environments. Bandura (1986) has called this type of event, when the outcome is favorable, a fortuitous event—that is, any life event (stressful or not) that opens up to a positive circumstance.

Sociocultural readiness factors. With the label *sociocultural readiness factors* we mean to draw attention to influences on developmental readiness that operate on a larger scale than the proximate environment of the individual.

Every society has developmental norms—ingrained standards, assumptions, rules, and expectations—for how, when, why, and to whom development (however defined) occurs. For example, the phenomenon of "decade age markers" discussed above points to a cultural norm which channels development. And we tend to make assumptions about what kind of developmental experiences are appropriate for old people versus young people—and what the age brackets of "old" and "young" are. Likewise, women and people of color have been subject to restrictions on their development based, partly, in assumptions about their potential. Recently, these restrictions have become more subtle but they have resulted nonetheless in "glass ceilings" and increased levels of poverty.

Thinking about developmental readiness requires that we examine such norms. We suggest that there are three ways in which developmental norms influence assessment of readiness. First, norms may produce undesirable barriers (for example, "glass ceilings") that may falsely characterize people as "not ready." Second, norms may accentuate feelings and perceptions of readiness in some cases (for example, "I'll be thirty next year; it's time to rethink my life."). Finally, cross-cultural differences in developmental norms can deeply complicate the assessment of readiness: How can I, as a person from the United States, understand what development—readiness, processes, outcomes—means to a native of Japan?

Also, what we have labeled as *social milieu* influences readiness. By social milieu, we mean the larger context of events and conditions in the society. For example, in the United States, the current upheaval of economic restructuring affects readiness for development, albeit in ways we do not understand very well. The overall social milieu has changed; each corporate restructuring is no longer an isolated event but an aspect of a social move-ment. Having experienced years of this movement, we know that downsizing may lead to trauma in those laid off and to "survivor sickness" among those remaining (Noer, 1993).

One useful way to frame such trauma or sickness is as a "neutral zone" (Bridges, 1988; see also 1980), a period in which prior meaning structures have been disrupted and new ones have not yet been found or consolidated. Understanding the inherent pain and dangers, Bridges cites ways in which this neutral zone can—or must—be used as a period of creativity, reflection, and renewal. In assessing readiness for development, it would be useful to understand the nature of not only the particular individual's neutral zone but the associated organizational and societal neutral zones as well. The chal-lenges for those of us contemplating leadership development are enormous: For example, how might we assess readiness for development in light of the neutral zones in the former Soviet republics?

Developmental Processes

By developmental processes, we are referring to *how* development occurs. How do individuals and systems evolve the capacity to make more encompassing, adaptive, and sufficiently complex meaning? Our model focuses on a particular aspect of leadership development processes: individu-als in programs. However, as the second box in the diagram of the model in Figure 2 illustrates, a leadership development program is embedded in a larger set of ongoing developmental processes with respect to workplace, family, social, and personal dynamics. Consideration of these "big picture" processes is vital in any developmental program aiming for a nontrivial impact on leadership.

According to our model, leadership development programs aim to provide an engaging experience, which produces disequilibrium in how the participants make meaning, which creates the potential for eventual reequilibration into a more encompassing and adaptive stage of being and behaving. A good program will provide and facilitate appropriate holding environments (including the functions of holding and letting go) for participants "where they are" (that is, the "old" stages) as well as for the emergent stages.

The program should provide support for an emerging set of meaning structures, while recognizing that the "new" equilibrium may be unstable, the often-tentative leading edge of a relatively slow and unsteady developmental movement. Thus, in our model, "regression" after the intervention is not necessarily seen as a failure of the intervention to properly transfer back to the real world. Rather, regression *along with* an increased potential for eventually stable new meaning structures is recognized as essential to the nature of developmental evolution. The recognition of this sort of potential is tricky, because potential is hard to observe, measure, or otherwise sense; this is where the readiness and outcomes portions of the model should prove useful.

According to our model, then, leadership development programs have five requisite, interwoven processes: experience, disequilibrium, equilibrium, construction, and potentiation.

Experience. Leadership development requires experience as one of its component processes. *Experience* as used here refers to circumstances that fully, broadly, and actively engage the person's meaning structures. Experience utilizes—and challenges—the depth and breadth of our abilities to construe the past, present, and future. What we mean by experience excludes, for example, purely rote learning, skill learning divorced from context, and circumstances in which the person is substantially hiding, disguising, or disengaging his usual mode of being.

A trainer from the LeaderLab program explains it this way: "When you're working with people's real-life experience—to me this is a key—you invite people to bring their 'real' selves in. Now, what does it mean to bring their real selves in? Well, I would say that it has a lot to do with their real-life experiences being invited to be front and center. Unfortunately, I think sometimes in our educational efforts we invite people to set aside their life experience and to take in some kind of abstract model" (R. M. Burnside, personal communication, October 18, 1994).

The idea that development requires the full engagement of life experiences (see also Dewey, 1963; James, 1890; Kegan, 1982; Kelly, 1955) can be contrasted with the idea that development is the *unfolding* of innate capacities (as expressed for example by Jaques & Clement, 1991, who maintain that leadership capacities develop according to a trajectory established at a very young age, if not in the womb) or is merely the *imprinting* of information via the senses onto a blank slate (as seen in much textbook and lecture-based training that takes a checklist approach to appropriate competencies). It may seem obvious that development results from an intense interaction between inner capacities and outer realities (Piaget, 1954), but this has often been ignored. And although the unfolding and imprinting perspectives have their place, they have too often been used as the primary engines in the pursuit of developmental goals.[5]

Leadership development in our view requires that individual and collective abilities to make effective sense of what's happening are at least occasionally stretched to the limit and beyond, in some context that provides for "holding" emergent new meaning structures. The trick for leadership development programs is to promote this kind of experience within the program constraints. Defining the role of the experience in this way puts such constraints in a new light, as illustrated in the case study in Appendix A.

Disequilibrium. Experience by itself is not enough for development. Everyday experience is quite often a rut—an engaging rut, to be sure, but a rut in that we tend to select and interpret experiences in line with our existing ways of understanding. The holding environment can conspire in this rut-making. Meaning structures tend to form self-confirming, self-sealing, apparently seamless wholes (Sullivan, 1953), rendering most experience familiar and tractable. However, the degree of clarity, and the apparent comprehensiveness which this condition provides, tends to preclude the evolution of new forms of meaning at more comprehensive and complex levels of adaptability—our definition of development.

Structures of meaning maintain equilibrium by efficiently assimilating and accommodating new experiences. Assimilation means interpreting new experience to fit one's existing meaning structures. When an experience does not fully assimilate, the meaning structures may accommodate; that is, they may stretch their forms (sometimes only temporarily) to take in the experience (Block, 1982, p. 286).

The metaphor Piaget used for equilibration is digestion: food (or an experience) is chewed up to fit the "digestive tract" of the organism (assimilation), while at the same time the "digestive tract" stretches and changes its "chemistry" (accommodation). At the conclusion of "digestion" the experience has been dealt with, and the person remains in balance without having changed in any substantial way. The belt comes out a notch but everything still fits, more or less. Minor accommodation acts to preserve rather than transform the essential structure.

Disequilibrium occurs when this routine of assimilation and accommodation becomes turbulent. The person attempting to take in an experience gets
"indigestion." The experience will not assimilate into the person's existing
framework, even with some stretching of the framework. Yet it cannot be
completely rejected as nonsense (labeling something as nonsense is a form of
assimilation). The facts don't behave. They don't all add up. Meaning gets
patched together, whereas before it was seamless. The experience is one of
loss of meaning, or confusion, and is frequently accompanied by feelings of
threat, anxiety, and pain. There may be anger at the messenger or agent of
the offending material. Interestingly, developmental disequilibrium may also
sometimes be experienced as exhilarating, as some combination of relief and
the sense of the onset of new possibilities.

This state of disequilibrium can be a most creative state, leading to the
potential for fundamental development (Bridges, 1988; Kelly, 1955;
Mezirow, 1991; Palus, 1993; Perry, 1981).

> There are few experiences in the biography of a man more distressing
> than that of feeling himself utterly confused. . . . The more deeply the
> confusion enters into my life the more alarmed I become. . . .
>
> Yet almost everything new starts in some moment of confusion.
> In fact, I cannot imagine just now how it could be otherwise. But this is
> not to say that confusion always serves to produce something new. It
> can just as well have the opposite effect, especially if the person finds
> the confusion so intolerable that he reverts to some older interpretation
> of what is going on. . . .
>
> But there is another stage in the creative process that stands
> midway between the confusion that we try to dispel by seeking either
> something new or regressing to something old, and the structured view
> of our surroundings that makes it appear that we know what's what. It is
> that transitional moment when the confusion has partly cleared and we
> catch a glimpse of what is emerging, but with it are confronted with the
> stark realization that we are to be profoundly affected if we continue on
> course. This is the moment of threat. It is the threshold between confu-
> sion and certainty, between anxiety and boredom. It is precisely at this
> moment when we are most tempted to turn back.
>
> Let us concentrate on this moment of threat—or these moments of
> threat—in the life of man. Let me suggest that if we can find some way
> of helping man pass this kind of crisis we will have helped him in one
> of the most important ways imaginable. (Kelly, 1969, pp. 151-152)

Equilibrium. Thus far we have established that leadership development programs provide experiences that disequilibrate meaning structures. Yet the experiences of living also do this (Kegan, 1982)—sometimes quite thoroughly in these days of organizational restructuring (Bridges, 1988; Noer, 1993)—and people often come to programs in considerable disequilibrium. The artful task of a program is to provide disequilibrium when necessary but also to provide timely and appropriate support and balance (equilibrium). This means appropriately affirming existing modes of being, as well as affirming newer, potentially more adaptive modes of being. A leadership development program thus has the difficult task of being a holding environment for both the old *and* the new, as well as acting as a medium of disequilibrium.

Not all developmental programs should be oriented toward the next stage of development. Piaget warned against the urge to accelerate the advent of the next stage (he called that urge "the American question"). Some participants in leadership development programs will have as their greatest developmental needs the affirmation and the continued exploration of their current stage of development. For example, a person at Kegan's (1982) "Institutional Stage" may still be building an autonomous identity and will need support in building awareness and confidence about the meaning structure of personal identity. "Going against the grain" as a learning strategy (Bunker & Webb, 1992)—that is, experimenting with experiences that appear to be counter to our own identity—must come after (or alongside) going with the grain—that is, learning in support of identity, "in line with" our character. "With the grain" learning is perhaps less likely to be an unsettling event than it is to be part of a flow along the lines of underlying strengths and proclivities. Although strengths that are used to excess eventually become weaknesses (McCall, Lombardo, & Morrison, 1988), developmentally it is necessary to first acquire those strengths.

Construction. Experience, equilibrium, and disequilibrium provide the necessary processes and contexts for development. What one *does* with these is critical. Simply experiencing, sensing, knowing, feeling, or reacting is not enough. Attention to the processes of making sense—making meaning—is essential.

> Developmentalists know something now about how to join the environment to stimulate development; but have we learned how to join or accompany the meaning-maker when he or she faces a world that is

already heated up, already stimulating, even to the point of being meaning-threatening?

> The greatest limit to the present model of developmental intervention is that it ends up being an address to a *stage* rather than a person, an address to made meanings rather than meaning-making. (Kegan, 1982, pp. 276-277, emphasis in original)

We believe that requisite leadership capacities for facing emerging challenges include the ability to take alternative perspectives and the ability to create, shape, and negotiate changed perspectives, both for oneself and within one's community (see the "Outcomes" section of this paper for more on this). In order to do this, one comes to an awareness that the imposing and seemingly unambiguous truth and reality of the world are substantially the result of our constructed perspectives, paradigms, and frameworks—and that these perspectives are not final but potentially open to various kinds of rebuilding.

Development is a journey; let's take a look at two highway signs. One is "Pedestrians Cross Here." Bridges (1988) points out that changing to a new set of meaning structures is often treated as if it were crossing a street and the goal only to get quickly to the other side. A more appropriate sign from our view is "Under Construction." It would be a mistake to think that the end is attained by crossing the street. There will always be streets to cross. Rather, adeptness with construction—with consciously visioning and revisioning, framing and reframing, personally and in community—is the real prize of leadership development.

Potentiation. Development, we believe, is not necessarily a uniform, linear, unidirectional progression through a sequence of meaning structures.[6] It has at least a bit of the swirling, stuttering movements that systems theorists have referred to as *chaos* (Wheatley, 1992). A linear motion would be the following: A person has a perspective, disequilibrates, and then finds a new and stable equilibration and a new perspective. More likely, a person disequilibrates, has some glimpse of or experience within a new perspective, and then *returns* to his or her original perspective—but with a greater potential for future movement along this newly created "fault line." Potentiation refers to the increased possibility of future sustained change in meaning structures. The person has been sensitized to the possibility that a meaning structure can in fact lose its ability to "make sense." Continued experience in the vicinity of this fault line increases the chances for additional glimpses of the new perspective until, eventually, a new structure of meaning develops and a new equilibration results. This will probably not happen as a result of a single leadership development program, of course. Such programs must be seen in the context of the overall role they play in a stream of disequilibrations that will be different for each person.

The loss of the glimpse of "a new meaning" may set up a kind of yearning to reengage the process of development. The experience of disequilibrium and reequilibration that are undergone in such an intervention often become a memory after a program, but a memory with important consequences for further evolution in the system of meaning-making. It can be part of the leading edge of a growing awareness of the possibility of a new, more adequate way of knowing. It is an important link in a chain of events that makes it successively more likely that a new way of knowing—and hence a new way of acting in the world—will be found. Perhaps, then, part of a program's power to foster development may be related to its power to stay in the memory.

William Perry (1970) offered an intriguing slant on developmental-stage potentiation in terms of a process he calls "the Trojan Horse." Perry observed that the Harvard undergraduate students he was studying would tend to make the transition from a comprehensively dualistic mode to a comprehensively relativistic mode[7] in a particular manner. Their professors would not reward their characteristic stage of "tell us the True Facts we should learn" (dualism) with good grades, instead requiring that they analyze and critique the utility of a variety of viewpoints (relativism). He also observed that at first the students would use relativism as a specific tool to approach assignments and tests for the purpose of getting a grade. Often they would use this tool quite well, albeit with cynicism. Their broader worldviews remained distinctly dualistic. Over the course of a year or two, however, the relativism would come out of where it had been lying in wait (as if from a Trojan Horse) and overcome the city. That is, the students would become relativistic in *many* of their affairs, scholarly, civic, relationships, and so on.

Thus, we extend the concept of potentiation to include the Trojan Horse. The "glimpse" of a new stage may be in the form of a useful tool, even if the stage represented in the tool is at first viewed with suspicion.

A leadership development program, to be most effective, should take some responsibility for actualizing the potential it creates. The lessons of the Trojan Horse, for example, do not support the idea that actualization of developmental potential unfolds automatically or without help. The elements of the intervention should include features such as long-term support systems, reconnection with fellow participants, follow-up (as opposed to one-shot deals), and ongoing activities begun during the program. Ideally, these features will be coordinated with those aspects of the organization and family-life holding environments that support development.

Safely taking risks in a leadership development program. We have discussed how leadership development must at some point threaten established ways of making meaning. Development can be seen as problematizing what was once taken for granted: "Probably . . . one should see the [developmental] sequence as one of coping with increasingly deeper problems rather than to see it as one of the successful negotiation of solutions" (Loevinger & Wessler, 1970, p. 7). Even when some new and more robust ways of making meaning are established by a person, feelings of loss can be profound: "It may be a great joy to discover a new and more complex way of thinking and seeing, but what do we do with all those hopes we had invested in those simpler terms (Perry, 1981)?" Those who run leadership development programs have a deep responsibility to address the risks involved, including maximizing the possibilities for beneficial outcomes, and obtaining informed consent from participants (Kaplan & Palus, 1994). Recognizing that programs differ greatly in focus and intensity, we consider the key points for maximizing the possibility for beneficial outcomes to be as follows:

Attention to readiness. The work in the program should be matched to the readiness of the participants. Participants should be assisted in self-selecting for the program based on an assessment of their own readiness for the work proposed. This means taking a "whole life" perspective on development—that is, being aware of possible influences of, and impacts on, personal, community, and family life as well as work life.

Equilibration. Attention must be given to appropriately stabilizing meaning structures, because much of the work of development involves disequilibrium—and extreme disequilibrium can be threatening, painful, and even harmful. The support capability of the participant's organization should be assessed, and work should be done to insure that the program fits in well with the other developmental initiatives of the organization.

Follow-up. Participants must be helped with getting back to their lives after having been put off-balance. They must be helped in identifying their own resources. The program itself should provide ongoing developmental resources. Other initiatives by the sponsoring organization should be in place to continue the work of development.

Outcomes

We have described leadership development as the increasing capacity to make encompassing and adaptive meaning in a community. We can list a number of meaning-making processes that, according to this perspective, are potential leadership processes: problem solving, questioning and suspending assumptions, relating, influencing, valuing, engaging in dialogue, telling stories, planning/acting/reflecting, framing, and creating environments. These, however, cannot be viewed simply as skills to be learned. Neither can we expect these to pop out in finished form at the end of a leadership development program. How can we best conceptualize the nature of the outcomes we might hope for?

Our model specifies four categories of potential outcomes for a leadership development program: (1) competencies and taking action; (2) meaning structures; (3) the particular kind of superordinate meaning structures we call developmental stages; and (4) holding environments. As Figure 2 indicates, these are nested: One's developmental stage frames other meaning structures, all of which frame competencies and action—all of which are supported (or not) by the holding environments. Each of these categories presents targets for development.

For example, taking action by going "against the grain" (or attempting to) can eventually lead to a change in developmental stage via the processes of experience, disequilibration, and potentiation. And vice versa: The equilibration of a new developmental stage makes it possible to take certain unaccustomed actions with a degree of integrity and competence (Drath, 1990).

Attention to each of these four categories is necessary in planning, implementing, following-up, and evaluating a leadership development program.

Competencies and taking action. The bottom line for any intervention is a significant increase in effective actions taken—for example, toward some goal or toward solving problems. The problem is that leadership requires facility with processes that cannot be treated as mere techniques, as if competencies were modular building blocks (Vaill, 1991). Truly effective empowerment, for example, is dependent on the long-term evolution in developmental stages and holding environments (Drath, 1990) and cannot normally be imparted as a competency (at least by the usual meanings of the word *competent*) during a leadership development program.

What *can* be done is to experiment with taking actions intending empowerment, see what happens, and then use the experiments to reveal and revise one's assumptions, biases, perspectives, and so on (that is, revise one's meaning structures). We call these reflective experiments with actions *developmental experiments*. Over the long term, developmental experiments may result in a new developmental stage and a step-change in the capacity to practice effective empowerment. During the course of such action-learning, we might reasonably hope that more—and more effective—action is taken.

Developmental programs in general are not expected to show broad, immediate transfer. What is expected to be carried back to the workplace is some facility for engaging the processes of development, including an experimental, reflective approach to taking action, and a better map of where these developmental experiments may lead.

Are there any competencies which a leadership development program might hope to impart by the end of a program? We believe that competencies having to do with *engaging the processes of action-learning and development in one's own world* are achievable by the end of a multiple-contact leadership development program. "The idea is that it's an experiment and you are the thing that is being experimented on and you are in charge of it" (R. M. Burnside, personal communication, October 18, 1994).

In general, these competencies include concepts and techniques for the enhancement of reflection, action planning, experimenting with new or improved actions in one's world, self-diagnosis and understanding, involving others in learning processes, and diagnosing and understanding one's holding environments. For example, LeaderLab participants learn how to keep journals as a tool for reflection; develop, test, and revise personal visions and action plans; and practice a holistic "head, heart, and feet" learning model. These learning competencies are pursued as tools in service of the long-term development of leadership capacities.

Thus, according to our model, if LeaderLab fails to immediately "transfer" the competencies it teaches (for instance, system thinking and maintaining flexibility) back to the workplace, it is not necessarily an indication that the program has not promoted development. In the words of one participant, "You can hear the song, but it may be that you're unable to sing the words yet. It's difficult."

Meaning structures. Leadership development programs help people acquire new, revised, and alternative ideas, maps, insights, and perspectives. These will almost certainly not be integrated immediately into a whole new developmental stage—neither will they easily assimilate into one's present stage of development (assuming the participant is matched with a program meant to challenge the person beyond his or her own present stage of making meaning). At first, these new meaning structures may be exercised as tools— with a longer-term potential of fostering a whole new way of looking at things (as discussed above with respect to the idea of potentiation and "the Trojan Horse").

For example, Senge (1990) describes systems thinking (in our present terms) as a new meaning structure. Systems thinking can be trained for and can be evaluated as an outcome. An individual can be formally and rigorously assessed on how well he or she can utilize the meaning structure of systems thinking. Per our model, the meaning structure of systems thinking can serve as a framework for increased competency in analyzing a situation and taking action. Beyond its use as a tool, systems thinking can become the basis for a new developmental epistemology, what Basseches (1984) calls "the dialectical mode."

Likewise, the meaning structure of total quality management (TQM) serves as a framework for taking action and can be fostered by the use of tools (such as fishbone diagrams). But it is important not to be obsessed by competency with tools as developmental outcomes. It is possible to acquire tools and still not "get it"—that is, still not be able to discern the underlying connections, values, and aims of total quality. It is quite possible that the Trojan Horse will be subjugated by the prior entrenched attitudes, rather than vice versa. Indeed, TQM often serves as a veneer over underlying *traditional* worldviews (Torbert, 1992).

Developmental stages. People undergoing a developmental experience at different points in transition will experience the program differently and have different outcomes (Lahey et al., 1985; Perry, 1981).

For a person in equilibrium within a stage, the outcome might be the temporary loss of balance associated with glimpsing the limits of that stage—with some potentiation for long-term movement in the same direction. Alternatively, if the program is set up such that it denies the participant's epistemology, then the outcome for the person might only be an indignant feeling of having wasted time.

For a person who has already begun to encounter the limits of a stage, the outcome might be frustration and confusion—and potentiation brought on by a full confrontation of those limits. William Perry (1981) described a dualistic-stage student enrolled in his "Strategies of Reading" course who expected to have Knowledge ladled out by an Authority. This was not at all Perry's style. Although the student improved immensely according to comparative scores on pre- and postcourse tests of reading speed and comprehension, he exhibited extreme frustration and apparent potentiation: "This has been the most sloppy, disorganized course I've ever taken. Of course I have made some improvement, but this has been due *entirely to my own efforts*" (p. 77, emphasis in original).[8]

For a person who has already begun to transcend a stage, the outcome might be the elation of discovering a new way to understand one's self and the world. Also, the outcome might include a need to affirm the new structure by denying or rejecting the older structure and its trappings.

Finally, a person who had already begun to deny an older stage might achieve a kind of awakening, coming fully into the new stage, and assimilating (rather than denying) the older stage. A person who achieves such an awakening might be able to offer a whole new mode of being to their work and to their organization. On the other hand, if the organization does not have a holding environment sufficient to sustain that person in his or her new stage of development, that person might feel compelled to leave (Bushe & Gibbs, 1990).

There are a number of methods available for assessing stage and stage changes. Such changes typically take place over a span of years (depending on what one defines as a stage) and usually cannot be attributed to specific programs or events (Kegan, 1982; Perry, 1981; Torbert, 1987). Yet according to our model, stage assessment can be useful for understanding and facilitating the overall course of development in an individual—including readiness, process, and outcomes. Methods of stage assessment include:

(1) The *Washington University Sentence Completion Test* (WUSCT). The WUSCT was developed by Jane Loevinger (Loevinger & Wessler, 1970) as a measure of stage of ego development. A version of the instrument was used by Torbert (1987) and his colleagues in their research, with different labels for the stages.

(2) A number of assessment methods have been developed using the Perry scheme for the assessment of stages of intellectual development. The Center for the Study of Intellectual Development offers a full range of services facilitating use of the Perry scheme.[9]

(3) Formal assessment of the Kegan stages of meaning-making and transitional substages requires training in the Subject-Object Interview methodology (Lahey et al., 1985).

(4) Michael Commons has developed a method for assessing stages of cognitive development from interview transcriptions (Commons & Richards, 1982).

(5) Michael Basseches (1984) has developed a method of assessing the use and coordination of dialectical schemata (although not primarily from a stage perspective).

Holding environments. The ability of environments—not just individuals—to hold and develop certain forms of meaning is essential to leadership development. Communities of practice are holding environments for leadership. According to our own view, we have emphasized individual development in this paper, and have said fairly little about how such an evolution of community would look like. One reason for this is that we at the Center have historically focused on individual development; we have paid relatively less attention to the evolution of processes of leadership as embedded in communities. However, our recent work in understanding, for example, dialogue, learning groups, total quality systems, and leadership as processes are efforts to broaden our view.

See Appendix A for an example of how readiness for development, developmental processes, and outcomes play out with an individual in a leadership development program.

Discussion and Implications

Our main themes in this report have been: Leadership development of individuals in programs is a matter of facilitating a shift to more encompassing and adaptive ways of knowing and experiencing a complex world; and development of this sort has myriad precedents and outcomes and tends to happen over long rather than short periods of time. In closing, we would like to emphasize a number of points related to these.

Leadership development is "whole life" in that it is vitally connected to family, personal, and community life, as well as work life—including the biographical aspects of each of these. Another way to say this: Leadership development is about the way a person broadly constructs, evolves, and enacts his or her values, relationships, memberships, and responsibilities.

Environments (such as organizations, families, and communities) may tend to promote stability within meaning systems more than evolution of meaning systems. This means that development of people without development of the holding environments may work against the development of both people and their contexts.

Leadership—meaning-making in communities of practice—is a set of processes that extend beyond the individual leader (although individual leaders are an important aspect of leadership processes). The purpose of working with individuals in programs is not to further concentrate leadership in those individuals. Rather, it is to build their abilities to foster and effectively participate in processes of leadership in their communities.

Leadership development is best considered over a span of years rather than (only) weeks and months. Short-term results from programs are possible and may be desirable, but the absence of obvious and dramatic short-term results does not necessarily indicate the absence of development. The pragmatics of outcome measurement have led to conceptions of development that emphasize the short term at the expense of understanding long-term development (see, for instance, Hellervik, Hazucha, & Schneider, 1992). Programs do best when they incorporate some form of long-term support and follow-up.

Development is largely a process of "getting outside the box" with respect to one's worldviews—and then getting outside that box—with "the box" being each sequential stage of development.

It is not enough to train for particular leadership competencies (Vaill, 1991). Holding environments, and stages of meaning-making, must also be developed if the competencies are to "take" and "make sense."

There are "inner" and "outer" approaches to assessing outcomes of development. The secret may lie in keeping our eye on both epistemologies *and* behaviors. If behaviors are manifested without an undergirding epistemology and suitable holding environment, they are very likely to be ephemeral. At the same time, it is new experience and experimentation with new behaviors—learning—that is a principal driver of epistemological evolution.

When we take these previous points together, it is clear that the process of leadership development is much larger than any single program or intervention. We therefore cannot speak of the outcomes of a particular program for an individual or for an organization without considering the larger context of systems, experiences, and circumstances. Leadership development of individuals in programs should therefore be coupled to systemic development of leadership processes in organizations.

There is a certain risk of pain, and even harm, to the individual and the organization, associated with development as described in this model (Kaplan & Palus, 1994). Evolving basic perspectives is unsettling at times, and it means moving from what is familiar into what is largely unknown. This risk may spill over into the family realm, as, for example, the individual takes new perspectives on the order of, "Who am I and what am I doing with my life?" Not everybody is ready for further disequilibration in the name of leadership development. Many people are already burdened with disequilibration on many fronts. Careful thought needs to be given to readiness: Who is ready for what kind of work?

There is a central developmental motion for a maturing leader that typically involves first developing a strong independent self-identity with which one can act with a high degree of confidence, authority, and autonomy. Further development involves the leader's being able to examine his or her system of beliefs as a system among many systems, and to surrender some autonomy and authority by redefining identity in terms of one's evolution as an individual in dialectical relationships in community—while at the same time not losing self-identity (Drath, 1990; Kegan, 1982).

The concept of "program" as traditionally defined is too limiting. Leadership development work needs to allow for individual tailoring (Boydell et al., 1991) and to be integrated into the routines of the organization.

Quite often the people in charge of organizations say they want to develop leadership within the organization ("How could that possibly be anything but good for the timely execution of our initiatives?"), but what they really mean is that they want people who are empowered to enact leadership that emanates from the top. Effective leadership development entails the creative risk that any sort of received wisdom will be questioned and even turned on its head. It invites some degree of apparent chaos, with staff choosing to go "under construction" rather than to obediently "cross the street." Choose carefully before you choose leadership development for your organization.

References

Baltes, P. B., Reese, H. W., & Lipsitt, L. P. (1980). Life-span developmental psychology. *Annual Review of Psychology, 31*, 65-110.

Bandura, A. (1986). *Social foundation of thought and action: A social cognitive theory.* Englewood Cliffs, NJ: Prentice-Hall.

Basseches, M. (1984). *Dialectical thinking and adult development.* Norwood, NJ: Ablex.

Block, J. (1982). Assimilation, accommodation, and the dynamics of personality development. *Child Development, 53*, 281-295.

Boydell, T., Leary, M., Megginson, D., & Pedler, M. (1991). *The developers: Improving the quality of the professionals who develop people and organizations.* London: Association for Management Education and Development.

Bridges, W. (1980). *Transitions: Making sense of life's changes.* Reading, MA: Addison-Wesley.

Bridges, W. (1988). *Surviving corporate transition: Rational management in a world of mergers, layoffs, start-ups, takeovers, divestitures, deregulation, and new technologies.* New York: Doubleday.

Bunker, K. A., & Webb, A. D. (1992). *Learning how to learn from experience: Impact of stress and coping* (Report No. 154). Greensboro, NC: Center for Creative Leadership.

Burnside, R. M., & Guthrie, V. A. (1992). *Training for action: A new approach to executive development* (Report No. 153). Greensboro, NC: Center for Creative Leadership.

Bushe, G. R., & Gibbs, B. W. (1990). Predicting organization development consulting competence from the Myers-Briggs Type Indicator and stage of ego development. *The Journal of Applied Behavioral Science, 26*(3), 337-357.

Commons, M. L., & Richards, F. A. (1982). A general model of stage theory. In M. L. Commons, F. A. Richards, & C. Armon (Eds.), *Beyond formal operations: Late adolescent and adult cognitive development.* New York: Praeger.

Costa, P. T., & McCrae, R. R. (1978). Objective personality assessment. In M. Storandt, I. C. Siegler, & M. F. Elias (Eds.), *The clinical psychology of aging.* New York: Plenum Press.

Dewey, J. (1963). *Experience and education.* New York: Collier.

Drath, W. H. (1990). Managerial strengths and weaknesses as functions of the development of personal meaning. *Journal of Applied Behavioral Science, 26*(4), 483-500.

Drath, W. H., & Palus, C. P. (1994). *Making common sense: Leadership as meaning-making in a community of practice* (Report No. 156). Greensboro, NC: Center for Creative Leadership.

Erikson, E. H. (1963). *Childhood and society* (2nd ed.). New York: Norton.

Gergen, K. J., & Gergen, M. M. (1987). The self in temporal perspective. In R. P. Abeles (Ed.), *Life-span perspectives and social psychology* (pp. 823-895). Hillsdale, NJ: Erlbaum.

Gilligan, C. (1982). *In a different voice: Psychological theory and women's development*. Cambridge, MA: Harvard University Press.

Gould, R. L. (1978). *Transformations: Growth and change in adult life*. New York: Simon & Schuster.

Heifetz, R. A. (1994). *Leadership without easy answers*. Cambridge, MA: Belknap Press.

Hellervik, L., Hazucha, J., & Schneider, R. (1992). Behavior models, methods, and review of evidence. In M. Dunnette & L. Hough (Eds), *Handbook of industrial and organizational psychology* (pp. 823-895). Palo Alto, CA: Consulting Psychologists Press.

James, W. (1890). *Principles of psychology*. New York: Henry Holt.

Jaques, E., & Clement, S. D. (1991). *Executive leadership*. Boston, MA: Basil Blackwell.

Kagan, J. (1971). *Change and continuity in infancy*. New York: Wiley.

Kaplan, R. E. (1990). *Character shifts: The challenge of improving executive performance through personal growth* (Report No. 143). Greensboro, NC: Center for Creative Leadership.

Kaplan, R. E. (1991). *The expansive executive* (2nd ed., Report No. 147). Greensboro, NC: Center for Creative Leadership.

Kaplan, R. E., Drath, W. H., & Kofodimos, J. R. (1985). *High hurdles: The challenge of executive self-development* (Report No. 135). Greensboro, NC: Center for Creative Leadership.

Kaplan, R. E., Drath, W. H., & Kofodimos, J. R. (1991). *Beyond ambition: How driven managers can lead better and live better*. San Francisco: Jossey-Bass.

Kaplan, R. E., & Palus, C. P. (1994). *Enhancing 360-degree feedback for senior executives: How to maximize the benefits and minimize the risks* (Report No. 160). Greensboro, NC: Center for Creative Leadership.

Kegan, R. (1982). *The evolving self*. Cambridge, MA: Harvard University Press.

Kegan, R. (1994). *In over our heads: The mental demands of modern life*. Cambridge, MA: Harvard University Press.

Kelly, G. A. (1955). *The psychology of personal constructs*. New York: Norton.

Kelly, G. A. (1969). The language of hypothesis: Man's psychological instrument. In B. Maher (Ed.), *Clinical psychology and personality: The selected papers of George Kelly* (pp. 147-162). New York: Wiley.

Kohlberg, L., & Kramer, R. (1969). Continuities and discontinuities in childhood and adult moral development. *Human Development, 12*, 93-120.

Korzybski, A. (1941). *Science and sanity: An introductions to non-Aristotelian systems and general semantics*. Lancaster, PA: The International Non-Aristotelian Library Publishing Company.

Lahey, L., Souvaine, E., Kegan, R., Goodman, R., & Felix, S. (1985). *A guide to the subject-object interview: Its administration and analysis*. Cambridge, MA: Subject-Object Research Group.

Lazarus, R. S. (1966). *Psychological stress and the coping process*. New York: McGraw-Hill.

Levinson, D. J., Darrow, C. N., Klein, E. B., Levinson, M. H.,& McKee, B. (1978). *The seasons of a man's life*. New York: Alfred A. Ballantine.

Loevinger, J. (1976). *Ego development*. San Francisco: Jossey-Bass.

Loevinger, J., & Wessler, R. (1970). *Measuring ego development, Volume 1*. San Francisco: Jossey-Bass.

McAdams, D. P. (1988). *Power, intimacy, and the life story*. New York: The Guilford Press.

McCall, M. W., Lombardo, M. M., & Morrison, A. M. (1988). *The lessons of experience: How successful executives develop on the job*. Lexington, MA: Lexington Books.

McCauley, C. D., Ruderman, M. N., Ohlott, P. J., & Morrow, J. E. (1994). Assessing the developmental components of managerial jobs. *Journal of Applied Psychology, 79*(4), 544-560.

McCrae, R. R., & Costa, P. T. (1984). *Emerging lives, enduring dispositions: Personality in adulthood*. Boston: Little, Brown.

McCrae, R. R., & Costa, P. T. (1990). *Personality in adulthood*. New York: The Guilford Press.

McCrae, R. R., & Costa, P. T. (in press). In Briggs, Jones, & Hogan (Eds.), *Handbook of personality psychology*. San Diego, CA: Academic Press.

Mezirow, J. (1991). *Transformative dimensions of adult learning*. San Francisco: Jossey-Bass.

Moore, W. S. (1989, November). The learning environment preferences; exploring the construct validity of an objective measure of the Perry scheme of intellectual development. *The Journal of College Student Development, 30*, 504-514.

Musselwhite, W. C. (1985). *The impact of timing on readiness to learn and transfer of learning from leadership development training: A case study*. Unpublished doctoral dissertation, North Carolina State University at Raleigh.

Noer, D. M. (1993). *Healing the wounds: Overcoming the trauma of layoffs and revitalizing downsized organizations*. San Francisco: Jossey-Bass.

Palus, C. J. (1993). Transformative experiences of adulthood: A new look at the seasons of life. In J. Demick, K. Bursick, & R. DiBiase (Eds.), *Parental development* (pp. 39-60). Hillsdale, NJ: Erlbaum.

Palus, C. J., Nasby W., & Easton, R. D. (1991). *Understanding executive performance: A life-story perspective* (Report No. 148). Greensboro, NC: Center for Creative Leadership.

Perry, W. G. (1970). *Forms of intellectual and ethical development in the college years: A scheme*. New York: Holt, Rinehart and Winston.

Perry, W. G. (1981). Cognitive and ethical growth: The making of meaning. In A. W. Chickering (Ed.), *The modern American college*. San Francisco: Jossey-Bass.

Piaget, J. (1954). *The construction of reality in the child*. New York: Basic Books.

Rest, J. R. (1979). *Development in judging moral issues*. Minneapolis, MN: University of Minnesota Press.

Rooke, D., & Torbert, W. R. (1995). *Organizational transformation as a function of the CEO's developmental stage*. Paper presented at the 1995 Academy of Management, Vancouver, BC.

Rybash, J. M. (1982). *Moral development during adulthood: The contributing influences of formal-operations and openess to experience.* Unpublished doctoral dissertation, Syracuse University.

Senge, P. M. (1990). *The fifth discipline.* New York: Doubleday.

Sheehy, G. (1976). *Passages: Predictable crises of adult life.* New York: Dutton.

Sullivan, H. S. (1953). *The interpersonal theory of psychiatry.* New York: Norton.

Taylor, S. E. (1989). *Positive illusions: Creative self-deception and the healthy mind.* New York: Basic Books.

Torbert, W. R. (1987). *Managing the corporate dream: Restructuring for long-term success.* Homewood, IL: Dow Jones-Irwin.

Torbert, W. R. (1991). *The power of balance.* London: Sage.

Torbert, W. R. (1992). The true challenge of generating continual quality improvement. *Journal of Management Inquiry, 1*(4), 331-336.

Vaill, P. B. (1991). *Managing as a performing art.* San Francisco: Jossey-Bass.

Van Velsor, E., & Musselwhite W. C. (1986, August). The timing of training, learning, and transfer. *Training and Development Journal*, pp. 58-59.

Wheatley, M. (1992). *Leadership and the new science: Learning about organization from an orderly universe.* San Francisco: Berrett-Koehler.

Winnicott, D. W. (1965). *The maturational processes and the facilitating environment.* New York: International Universities Press.

Young, D. P., Palus, C. J., & Dixon, N. M. (1993, June 25-27). *Readiness, process, and outcomes of an intensive leadership development program.* Paper presented at the Eighth Annual Symposium of the Society for Research in Adult Development, Amherst, MA.

Appendix A
A Case Example of Applying the Model to an Individual in a Development Program

To illustrate how elements of our model (see Figure A1)—readiness, developmental processes, and outcomes—play out in a leadership development program, we use examples here drawn from a program offered by the Center for Creative Leadership. LeaderLab® (see Burnside & Guthrie, 1992; Young et al., 1993) is a six-month-long, extended-contact program. It begins with one week of class time at the Center, followed by three months of action and application at the workplace. Participants then return to the Center for another week of class time, followed by another two and a half months of action and application.

Throughout the six months a Center-employed "consultative coach" called a *process advisor* is assigned to work one-on-one with the participant. Participants also select a co-worker, called a *change partner*, to assist them as they implement action plans developed in the program. A guiding idea of the program is "head, heart, and feet"—indicating the values of an intellectual understanding of one's leadership situation ("head"), an emotionally satisfying integration of life pursuits ("heart"), and appropriately changing behavior and taking action ("feet").

The case materials we use below have been disguised to ensure confidentiality.

Readiness

Tony Smith is a senior manager in a manufacturing organization we will call ABC Co. In what sense was he ready—or not—to participate in LeaderLab?

ABC had reorganized in order to emphasize team, rather than individual, performance. Smith did not have the requisite team skills or attitudes. He was, in fact, the opposite of a team player: abrasive, aggressive, always setting things up for a win-lose situation so that he could win. He would do his homework up to the wee hours of the night in order to hammer one of his peers the next day at a meeting. He had gotten a lot of feedback about this, from his boss, from his team, and from an internal consultant. His boss would not support Smith for any advancement in the organization. Smith was also in some personal pain, having been estranged from his two adult children for several years. He had tried psychological therapy. Things really weren't working for him and he knew it. He had tried to change without much success. Before the program, he said, "I feel as if this is make-it-or-break-it time." He was very explicit about what he needed to work on and why.

In Smith's profile we can see a high level of readiness to engage in developmental work. His considerable ambition had become painfully bounded by his habitual behaviors and attitudes. His work environment offered a certain level of affirmation about his accomplishment. The environment provided adequate feedback and support but demanded further development. His company was being fairly clear that it was serious about expecting a new set of team competencies as criteria for advancement. He was at an age—forty—when society almost expects a psychological transition. Smith himself had become more open to change and had expressed willingness to do hard work, to "make it or break it."

Developmental Processes

Experience. LeaderLab is experiential in two ways. First, it uses the participants' worklife and, to some self-selective degree, personal life as its materials for action and reflection. For example, each participant receives the results of 360-degree feedback (from peers, superiors, and subordinates) early in the program; this informs an action plan that is then tested in the workplace and revised during the second in-residence session of the program. Second, it uses self-contained experiential elements. For example, participants are selected to represent a diversity of backgrounds. Coupled with elements emphasizing group interaction and self-expression, this typically leads to the kind of comprehensive engagement of values, attitudes, assumptions, and so on that signify experience.

In the case of Tony Smith, although he had heard some of the critical messages given in feedback to him before, the program provided the support necessary to reflect on them. He was able to bring the issues contained in his feedback into the events of the program, to reflect and work on the issues, thereby turning those events into valid developmental experiences.

Participants are asked to keep journals when they return home, and Tony Smith would sometimes stay at his office until midnight journaling. He overdid it, just as he did everything else in his life, but he was still able to use that tool to see what was going on with himself. For example, in this journaling he wrote about his wife's concern that he was changing and that she didn't feel part of the change process. The process of development in programs can be expected to interact with meaning-making in real-life experience. As in many such cases, Smith's spouse was drawn into the dynamics of the leadership development program.

Disequilibrium and equilibrium. Tony Smith entered LeaderLab with a high level of pain and anxiety. Fear became added to these emotions as he began the program work. The case observer reported that "it was real frightening because the changes he was working on were changes that were affecting him at home too." Tony Smith also found a variety of sources of equilibrium in his development work. The LeaderLab process advisor is a kind of personal coach. In Tony's case, that relationship came to work fairly well: affirming him, encouraging him, helping him to remember what his strengths were—not just focusing on his weaknesses.

Construction. Tony Smith was working on constructing his world in new ways—that is, he looked at the ways he thought about and engaged his world and how those might evolve. One of these was a nagging sense of his own inferiority. With his process advisor, Tony worked out a more balanced self-appraisal that helped him think about his strengths and weaknesses in a more hopeful way. In order to make and sustain changes, he had to look at his role in the organization differently, and he had to understand what a team really is. This involved giving and getting information in new ways. In the words of the case observer, "He flew around the country and met one-on-one with every peer, and he actually said to them, 'This is what I have learned about myself in going through this process. Here's who I really am; here are the things that I am trying to work on, that I have made a commitment to try and change. I need your help in that process. Will you work with me? Will you give me feedback? Will you call me on it when you see me doing the old behaviors? Are you willing to be a partner? I really need you.'"

Potentiation. Like many program participants, Tony reverted back to his "old ways" in the months after the program. Underlying meaning structures are slow to change. With respect to potentiation, the key question is: "Has a seed been planted, and is the seed alive and growing?" In talking with Tony a year later, we saw an enhanced potential for further development: "I'm still hard on people in meetings too often, but I catch myself. Sometimes I catch myself during a meeting, and I back off. Before, I had no idea, really, of my harsh effect on people. Now I have this bigger idea about how teams work and that excites me, even though I don't always live up to it. It makes sense to me now. I think I'm making progress."

Outcomes

Using the model, we can see a set of nested outcomes for Tony. At the broadest level, Tony is working on a new stage of development. This stage is one in which his relationships are no longer automatic but rather are based on a clearer self-identity and an honest sense of his own strengths and weaknesses. Within this new stage, Tony is able to use the meaning structure of teamwork: that is, he sees himself as being able to make informed choices about his roles and the way he relates in teams. At the level of actions, Tony has become less impulsive. He asks more questions in meetings. A year later, one peer said to us: "He no longer bangs his fist on the table and shouts 'This is how it is!'"

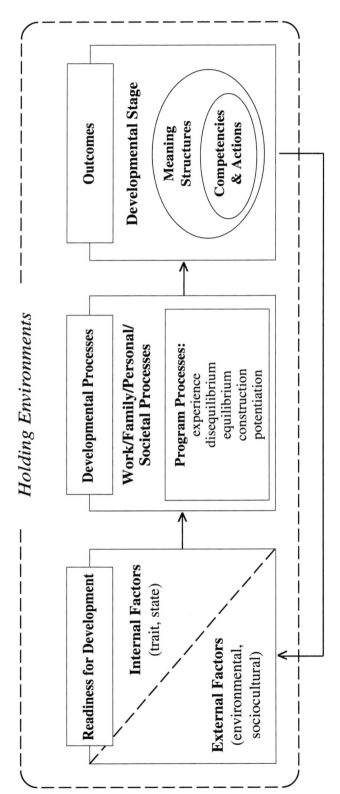

Figure A1. Leadership Development Program Model

Appendix B
Example of One Concept of Stages of Development

XYZ is a manufacturing company operating worldwide. (We have disguised identifying details.) Several years ago the CEO decided to send its top levels of management through the Center's Leadership Development Program (LDP). The first author of this report has been involved in a study of this use of LDP in the context of all of XYZ's organization-development processes. Here we briefly present that case in light of our model.

The development of the leaders within XYZ can be described as a progression of developmental stages. We call those stages *Dependency*, *Independency*, and *Interdependency*; these are roughly consistent with (in order) Stage 3, Stage 4, and Stage 5 described by Kegan (1982). Some characteristics of these stages are shown in Figure B1 (p. 40).

Readiness

First, consider the influence of the environment on readiness for development. A few years before we started our study, a new CEO was hired from outside the industry. Among his first actions was a reorganization of top management, followed by the study and implementation of a number of badly needed management systems, under the larger frame of a quality certification. Soon after, a number of organization-development initiatives were started, including a clarification of company values, climate surveys, and a system of periodic mutual feedback in groups.

In retrospect, the organization was changing from requiring loyalty and adherence to tradition from its managers, to requiring them to be independent operators of a set of rational management systems. Managerial performance criteria were changing accordingly. Our measures (using the *Washington University Sentence Completion Test*) of the developmental positions of these managers before LDP indicated that most were at the transition between Stage 3 and Stage 4.

Our overall diagnosis of readiness is that most of the managers were ready for the kind of Stage 4 meaning structures fostered by LDP. Just as important, the initiatives being implemented by the company were highly compatible with LDP.

Developmental Processes

LDP emphasizes self- and other-awareness as a means of consciously practicing leadership. One of the major in-program tools is reflection on

Figure B1. Development at XYZ

	Individual Manifestation		*Organizational Manifestation*
Stage	**Potential Strengths**	**Potential Weaknesses**	
3: DEPENDENCE	loyalty; mutual understanding; traditionally valued competencies; ease of interaction due to shared values and goals	overdependence on company; lack of independent initiative; can't see outside the local culture; not self-reflective	orientation to long-standing taken-for-granted traditions and values
4: INDEPENDENCE	exercise independent authority and responsibility; rational, systematic analysis; self-reflective	self-protective; overly ambitious; overly bound to systems and procedures; difficulty with close relationships	reworking traditions in light of rational systems, e.g., quality, finance, info technology, logistics
5: INTERDEPEN-DENCE	independent authority becomes subordinate to processes of mutual growth; can facilitate complex change; helps self and others learn; challenges own assumptions; engages in constructive conflict; self-objective	less driven by work; disruptive; too change-oriented; indecisiveness due to seeing many sides of issues	forming partnerships with other organizations; enhanced need for global communication; need to become more nimble, creative, and adaptive

feedback from work colleagues and from psychological test instruments. Support is given for developing an independent, authoritative, and systemic point of view, while still respecting the various "dependencies" or memberships the person has within work, family, and the community. XYZ managers reported substantial learning from fellow LDP participants representing very different types of industries. These processes are consistent with a Stage 3 to Stage 4 transition.

Outcomes

Participants tended to exhibit change in the following areas: They became more adept at relationships with colleagues. They worked harder at achieving a satisfying balance between their jobs and their families. They found it easier to "stand up" to top management in asserting their points of view. They became more comfortable with the new systems of management as a positive evolution of the traditions of their business. These outcomes are consistent with movement from Stage 3 to Stage 4.

It is important to note that developmental processes and outcomes are not limited to those caused by LDP. Organization-development systems in this case reinforced the developmental processes and desired outcomes of the program. There are also other factors, including individual managers' life stage and family transitions, which have contributed to their changes.

Because of the organization-development contribution, it seems appropriate to extend our stage analysis to the organizational level of development. The right-hand column of Figure B1 shows our interpretation of the organizational manifestation of stage development (this is consistent with the work of Torbert, 1987, and colleagues—Rooke & Torbert, 1995). We believe that this company as a whole is evolving into the meaning structure of Independence. But there are also indications that Interdependence is being increasingly called for. This brings us back around in the model to readiness: Further leader development in the company should begin to look for and strengthen signs of readiness in managers to take on an Interdependence framework.

Notes

1. This has been called a strong model of development; see Baltes, Reese, and Lipsitt (1980). Piaget, and later Kohlberg and others, have laid out strong-view criteria for human developmental stages (Kohlberg & Kramer, 1969).

2. The stages in this example may seem at first not to exemplify meaning. However, as Piaget (1954) points out, an infant makes sense of the world largely in terms of his or her own movements and raw sensation (the "sensory-motor stage").

3. Our main source and inspiration for the neo-Piagetian approach in this paper is Robert Kegan (1982, 1994), whose ideas integrate current ideas in the field about mature adult development. Other compatible frameworks include those of Erikson (1963), Gilligan (1982), Kohlberg and Kramer (1969), Loevinger (1976), and Perry (1970). Basseches (1984) provides a powerful perspective on similar themes which is *not* based in stage theory and which serves as a needed counterpoint. Torbert (1987) and Boydell, Leary, Megginson, and Pedler (1991) have done much work in applying such ideas to organizational settings.

4. The term *meaning* in this paper refers to the construal of order by all modes in which people apprehend the world, including social relationships, emotion, logic, the arts, and intuition. We do not limit meaning to only cognitive understanding. The term *structures* refers to the patterns and connections that tie meaning together at both small scales (for instance, personal stories) and large scales (for instance, cultural ideologies). Thus, the meaning structures of most interest in this paper are developmental epistemologies.

5. Bill Torbert (1991) has been a pioneer in redesigning university business administration programs along experiential lines, with stage development as the explicit goal.

6. We realize that the preceding discussion has emphasized linear progression. This is the conceptual price one pays for using simplifying models.

7. Perry actually distinguishes many substeps within what what is commonly referred to as *relativism*, including a final stage called *committed relativism* which does not succumb to the pejorative "every idea is equally valid." Here we are lumping those into the term *relativism* for simplicity in the presentation of the idea of the Trojan Horse.

8. Notice from this example that learning can take place alongside of, or in service of, development. Here we are focusing on the evolution of *how* things are learned, rather than assessing outcomes in terms of learning content.

9. Information on CSID is available from William S. Moore, Ph.D., 1520 14th Ave. SW, Olympia, WA 98502, 206/786-5094.

CENTER FOR CREATIVE LEADERSHIP PUBLICATIONS

SELECTED REPORTS:

Beyond Work-Family Programs J.R. Kofodimos (1995, Stock #167) $25.00
CEO Selection: A Street-Smart Review G.P. Hollenbeck (1994, Stock #164) $25.00
Coping With an Intolerable Boss M.M. Lombardo & M.W. McCall, Jr. (1984, Stock #305) $10.00
The Creative Opportunists: Conversations with the CEOs of Small Businesses
J.S. Bruce (1992, Stock #316) $12.00
Creativity in the R&D Laboratory T.M. Amabile & S.S. Gryskiewicz (1987, Stock #130) $12.00
Eighty-eight Assignments for Development in Place: Enhancing the Developmental
Challenge of Existing Jobs M.M. Lombardo & R.W. Eichinger (1989, Stock #136) $15.00
Enhancing 360-degree Feedback for Senior Executives: How to Maximize the Benefits and
Minimize the Risks R.E. Kaplan & C.J. Palus (1994, Stock #160) $15.00
An Evaluation of the Outcomes of a Leadership Development Program C.D. McCauley &
M.W. Hughes-James (1994, Stock #163) $35.00
Evolving Leaders: A Model for Promoting Leadership Development in Programs C.J. Palus &
W.H. Drath (1995, Stock #165) $20.00
Feedback to Managers, Volume I: A Guide to Evaluating Multi-rater Feedback Instruments
E. Van Velsor & J. Brittain Leslie (1991, Stock #149) $20.00
Feedback to Managers, Volume II: A Review and Comparison of Sixteen Multi-rater
Feedback Instruments E. Van Velsor & J. Brittain Leslie (1991, Stock #150) $80.00
Gender Differences in the Development of Managers: How Women Managers Learn From
Experience E. Van Velsor & M. W. Hughes (1990, Stock #145) $35.00
A Glass Ceiling Survey: Benchmarking Barriers and Practices A.M. Morrison, C.T. Schreiber,
& K.F. Price (1995, Stock #161) $20.00
High Hurdles: The Challenge of Executive Self-Development R.E. Kaplan, W.H. Drath, &
J.R. Kofodimos (1985, Stock #125) $15.00
The Intuitive Pragmatists: Conversations with Chief Executive Officers J.S. Bruce
(1986, Stock #310) $12.00
Key Events in Executives' Lives E.H. Lindsey, V. Homes, & M.W. McCall, Jr.
(1987, Stock #132) $65.00
Leadership for Turbulent Times L.R. Sayles (1995, Stock #325) $20.00
Learning How to Learn From Experience: Impact of Stress and Coping K.A. Bunker &
A.D. Webb (1992, Stock #154) $30.00
Making Common Sense: Leadership as Meaning-making in a Community of Practice
W.H. Drath & C.J. Palus (1994, Stock #156) $15.00
Off the Track: Why and How Successful Executives Get Derailed M.W. McCall, Jr., &
M.M. Lombardo (1983, Stock #121) $10.00
Preventing Derailment: What To Do Before It's Too Late M.M. Lombardo &
R.W. Eichinger (1989, Stock #138) $25.00
The Realities of Management Promotion M.N. Ruderman & P.J. Ohlott (1994, Stock #157) $20.00
Redefining What's Essential to Business Performance: Pathways to Productivity,
Quality, and Service L.R. Sayles (1990, Stock #142) $20.00
Succession Planning L.J. Eastman (1995, Stock #324) $20.00
Training for Action: A New Approach to Executive Development R.M. Burnside &
V.A. Guthrie (1992, Stock #153) $15.00
Traps and Pitfalls in the Judgment of Executive Potential M.N. Ruderman & P.J. Ohlott
(1990, Stock #141) $20.00
Twenty-two Ways to Develop Leadership in Staff Managers R.W. Eichinger & M.M. Lombardo
(1990, Stock #144) $15.00
Upward-communication Programs in American Industry A.I. Kraut & F.H. Freeman
(1992, Stock #152) $30.00
Using an Art Technique to Facilitate Leadership Development C. De Ciantis (1995, Stock #166) ... $30.00
Why Executives Lose Their Balance J.R. Kofodimos (1989, Stock #137) $20.00

Why Managers Have Trouble Empowering: A Theoretical Perspective Based on Concepts of Adult Development W.H. Drath (1993, Stock #155) $15.00

SELECTED BOOKS:

Balancing Act: How Managers Can Integrate Successful Careers and Fulfilling Personal Lives J.R. Kofodimos (1993, Stock #247) $27.00

Beyond Ambition: How Driven Managers Can Lead Better and Live Better R.E. Kaplan, W.H. Drath, & J.R. Kofodimos (1991, Stock #227) $29.95

Breaking the Glass Ceiling: Can Women Reach the Top of America's Largest Corporations? (Updated Edition) A.M. Morrison, R.P. White, & E. Van Velsor (1992, Stock #236A) $12.50

Choosing to Lead K.E. Clark & M.B. Clark (1994, Stock #249) $35.00

Developing Diversity in Organizations: A Digest of Selected Literature A.M. Morrison & K.M. Crabtree (1992, Stock #317) $25.00

Discovering Creativity: Proceedings of the 1992 International Creativity and Innovation Networking Conference S.S. Gryskiewicz (Ed.) (1993, Stock #319) $30.00

Executive Selection: A Look at What We Know and What We Need to Know D.L. DeVries (1993, Stock #321) $20.00

Healing the Wounds: Overcoming the Trauma of Layoffs and Revitalizing Downsized Organizations D.M. Noer (1993, Stock #245) $26.00

If I'm In Charge Here, Why Is Everybody Laughing? D.P. Campbell (1980, Stock #205) $9.40

If You Don't Know Where You're Going You'll Probably End Up Somewhere Else D.P. Campbell (1974, Stock #203) $8.95

Inklings: Collected Columns on Leadership and Creativity D.P. Campbell (1992, Stock #233) $15.00

Leadership Education 1994-1995: A Source Book F.H. Freeman, K.B. Knott, & M.K. Schwartz (Eds.) (1994, Stock #322) $59.00

Leadership: Enhancing the Lessons of Experience R.L. Hughes, R.C. Ginnett, & G.J. Curphy (1992, Stock #246) $40.95

The Lessons of Experience: How Successful Executives Develop on the Job M.W. McCall, Jr., M.M. Lombardo, & A.M. Morrison (1988, Stock #211) $22.95

Making Diversity Happen: Controversies and Solutions A.M. Morrison, M.N. Ruderman, & M. Hughes-James (1993, Stock #320) $25.00

Measures of Leadership K.E. Clark & M.B. Clark (Eds.) (1990, Stock #215) $59.50

The New Leaders: Guidelines on Leadership Diversity in America A.M. Morrison (1992, Stock #238) $29.00

Readings in Innovation S.S. Gryskiewicz & D.A. Hills (Eds.) (1992, Stock #240) $25.00

Take the Road to Creativity and Get Off Your Dead End D.P. Campbell (1977, Stock #204) $8.95

Whatever It Takes: The Realities of Managerial Decision Making (Second Edition) M.W. McCall, Jr., & R.E. Kaplan (1990, Stock #218) $30.40

The Working Leader: The Triumph of High Performance Over Conventional Management Principles L.R. Sayles (1993, Stock #243) $24.95

SPECIAL PACKAGES:

Conversations with CEOs (includes 310 & 316) $16.00

Development & Derailment (includes 136, 138, & 144) $30.00

The Diversity Collection (includes 145, 236, 238, 317, & 320) $85.00

Executive Selection Package (includes 141, 321, & 157) $32.00

Feedback to Managers: Volumes I & II (includes 149 & 150) $85.00

Personal Growth, Taking Charge, and Enhancing Creativity (includes 203, 204, & 205) $20.00

Discounts are available. Please write for a comprehensive Publication & Products Catalog. Address your request to: Publication, Center for Creative Leadership, P.O. Box 26300, Greensboro, NC 27438-6300, 910-545-2805, or fax to 910-545-3221. All prices subject to change.

ORDER FORM

Name _____ Title _____

Organization _____

Mailing Address _____
(street address required for mailing)

City/State/Zip _____

Telephone _____ FAX _____
(telephone number required for UPS mailing)

Quantity	Stock No.	Title	Unit Cost	Amount

Subtotal	
Shipping and Handling (add 6% of subtotal with a $4.00 minimum; add 40% on all international shipping)	
NC residents add 6% sales tax; CA residents add 7% sales tax; CO residents add 6.2% sales tax	
TOTAL	

METHOD OF PAYMENT

❑ Check or money order enclosed (payable to Center for Creative Leadership).

❑ Purchase Order No. _____ (Must be accompanied by this form.)

❑ Charge my order, plus shipping, to my credit card:
       ❑ American Express ❑ Discover ❑ MasterCard ❑ VISA

ACCOUNT NUMBER: _____ EXPIRATION DATE: MO.____ YR.____

NAME OF ISSUING BANK: _____

SIGNATURE _____

❑ Please put me on your mailing list.
❑ Please send me the Center's quarterly newsletter, *Issues & Observations.*

Publication • Center for Creative Leadership • P.O. Box 26300
Greensboro, NC 27438-6300
910-545-2805 • FAX 910-545-3221

                          Client Priority Code: R

fold here

_____

_____

_____

CENTER FOR CREATIVE LEADERSHIP
PUBLICATION
P.O. Box 26300
Greensboro, NC 27438-6300